# COW COLORING BOOK FOR ADULTS

## Stress-relief Coloring Book For Grown-ups, Containing 40 Paisley, Henna and Mandala Style Coloring Pages

By
Coloring Books Now

Copyright © 2016 Coloring Books Now
All Rights Reserved.

ISBN-13: 978-1539086963

ISBN-10: 1539086968

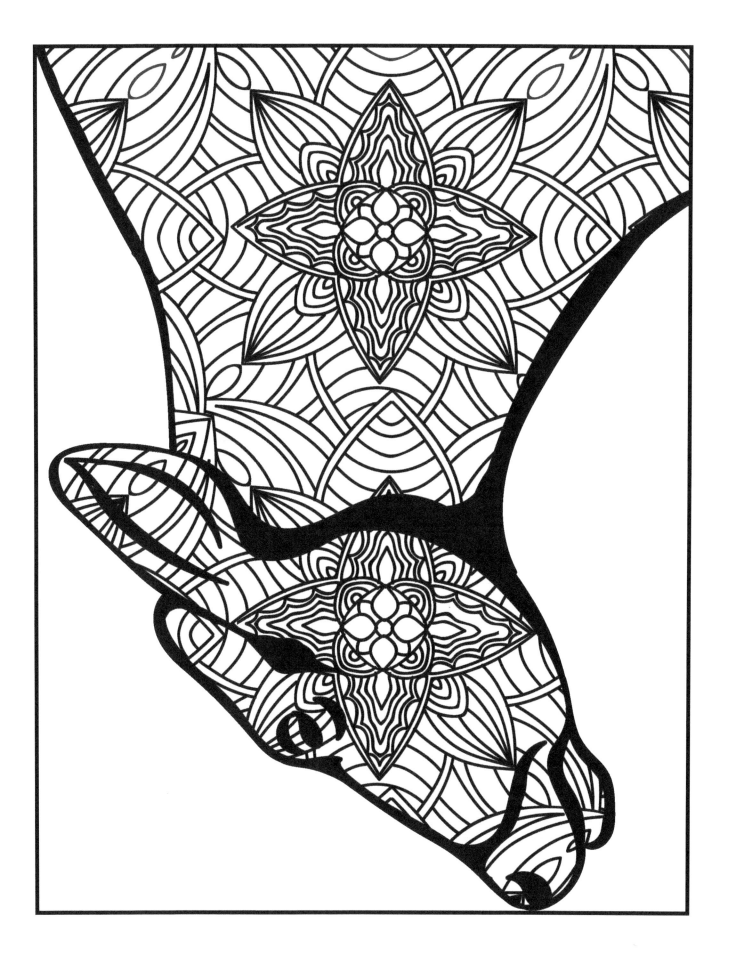

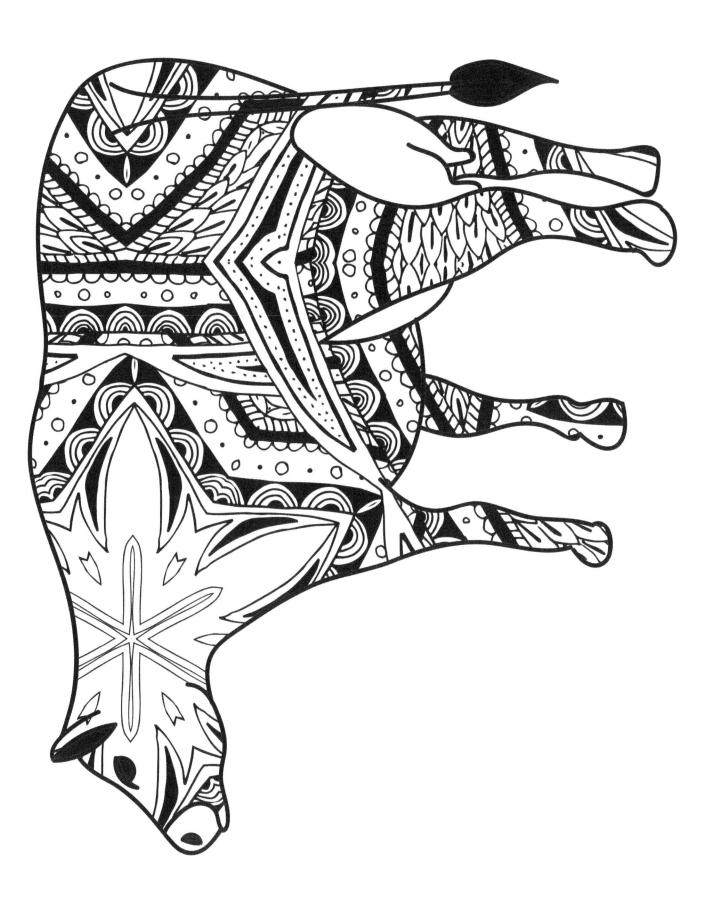

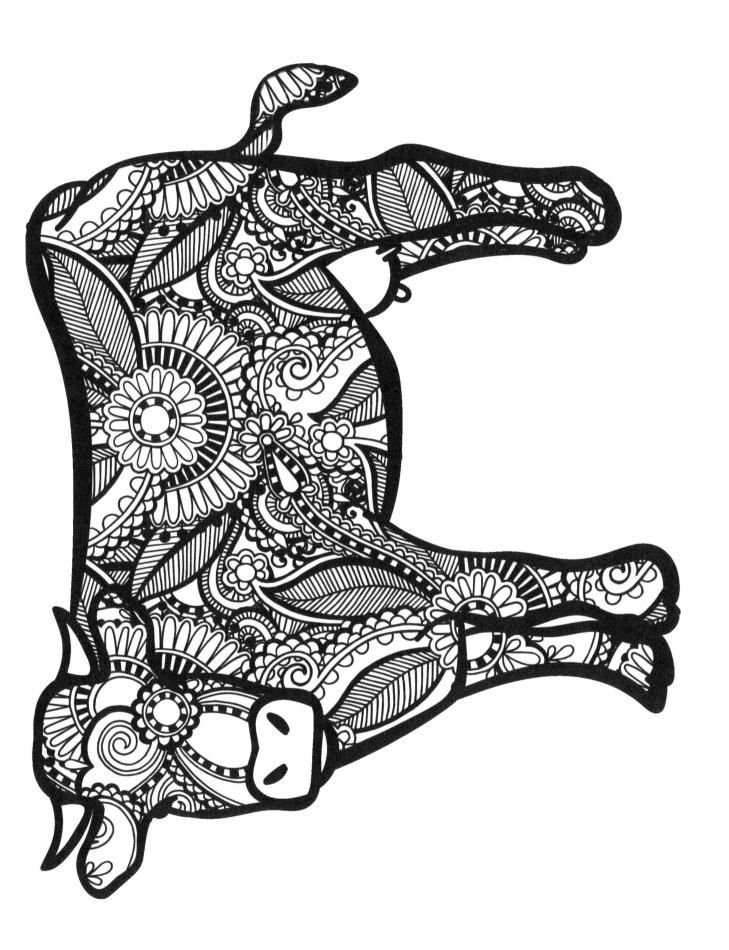

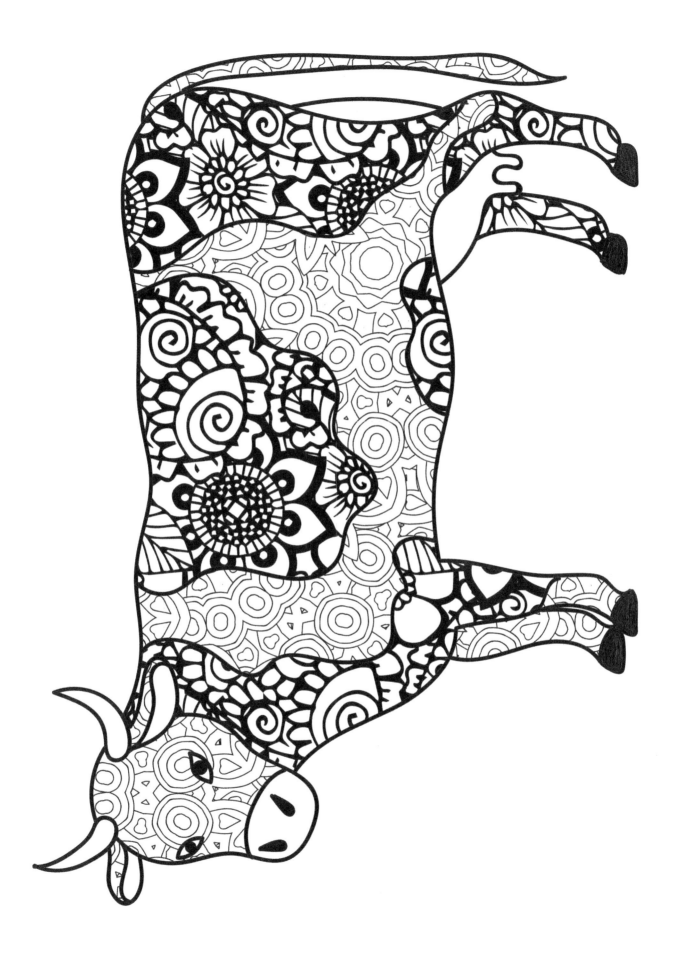

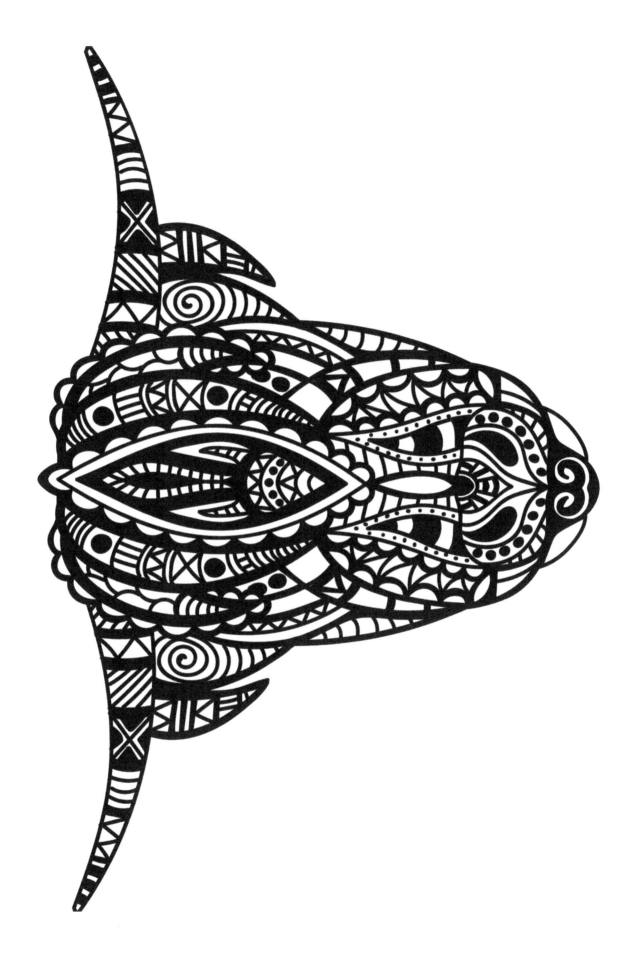

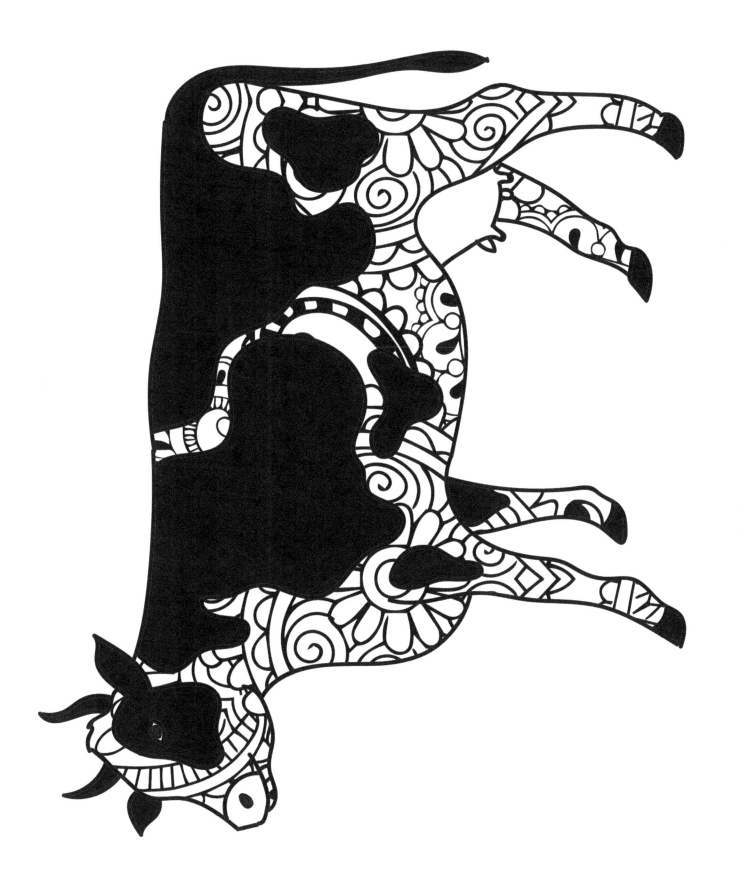

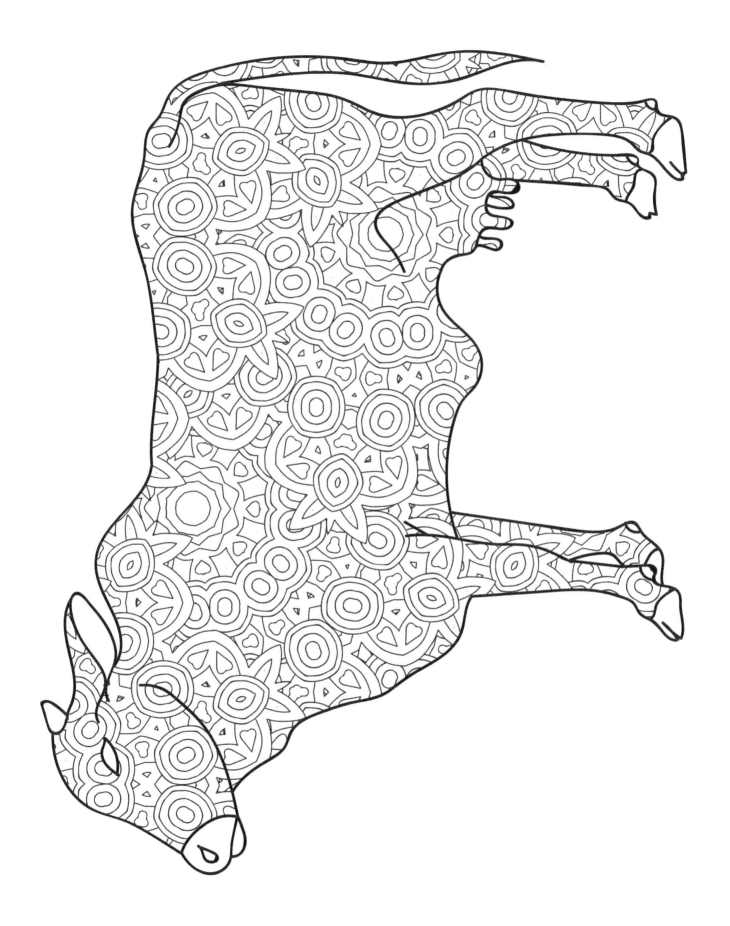

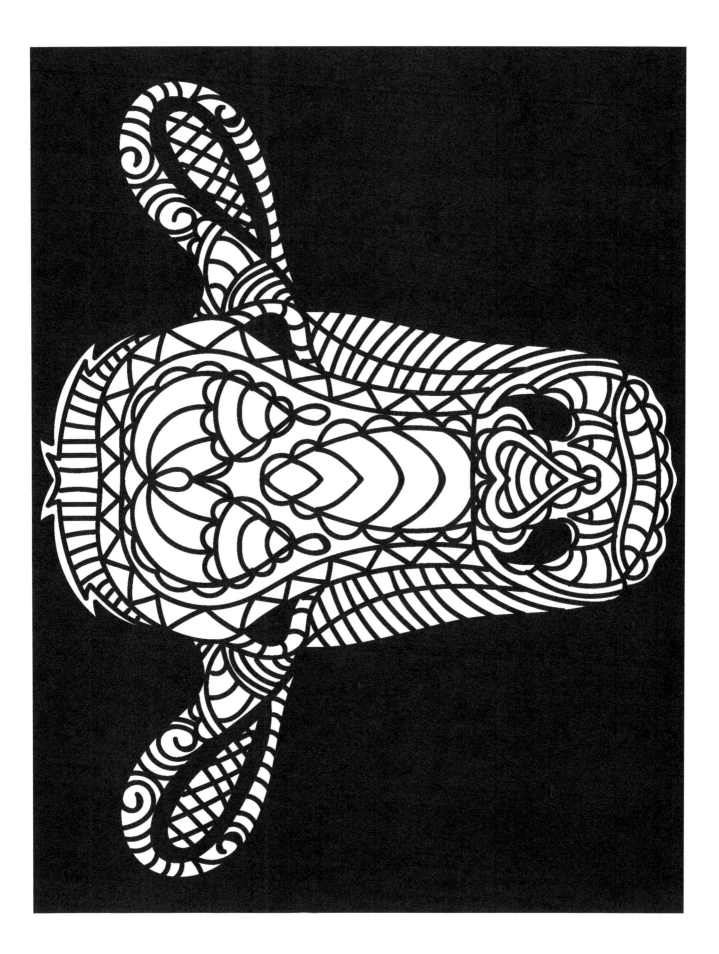

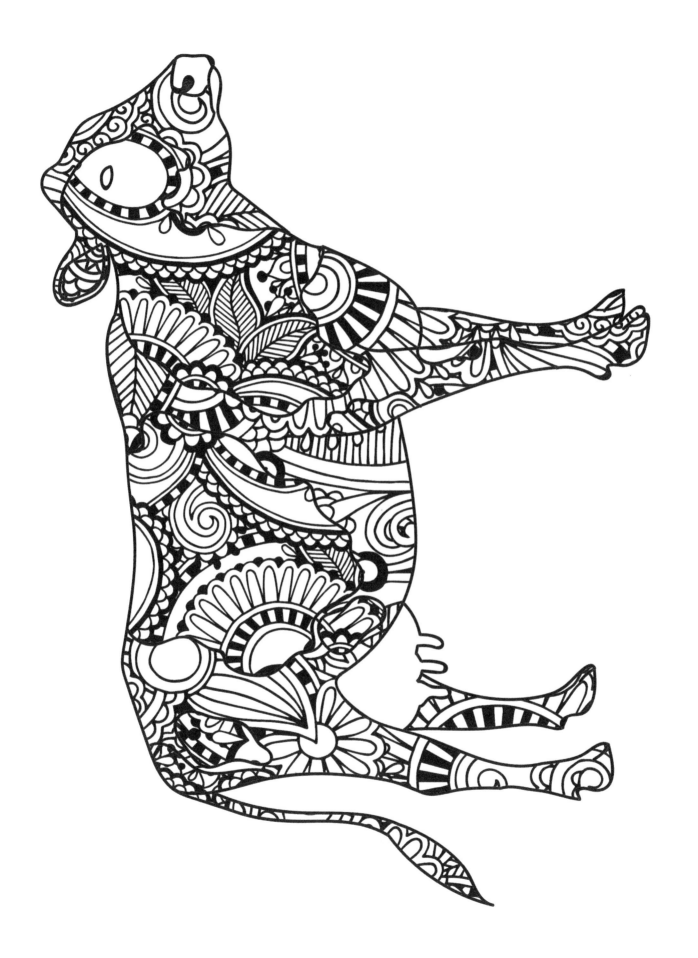

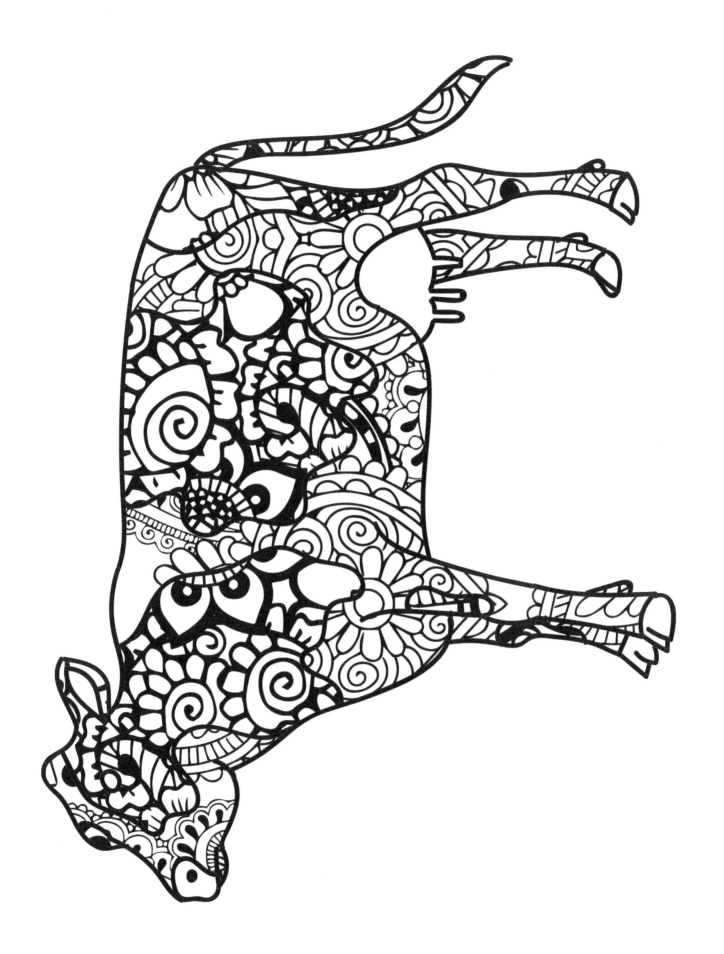